★ELTON JOHN

A Little Golden Book® Biography

By Jennifer Dussling

Illustrated by Irene Chan

A GOLDEN BOOK • NEW YORK

Text copyright © 2024 by Jennifer Dussling
Cover art and interior illustrations copyright © 2024 by Irene Chan
All rights reserved. Published in the United States by Golden Books, an imprint of Random
House Children's Books, a division of Penguin Random House LLC, 1745 Broadway,
New York, NY 10019. Golden Books, A Golden Book, A Little Golden Book, the G colophon,
and the distinctive gold spine are registered trademarks of Penguin Random House LLC.
rhcbooks.com
Educators and librarians, for a variety of teaching tools, visit us at RHTeachersLibrarians.com
Library of Congress Control Number: 2023930085
ISBN 978-0-593-64730-1 (trade) — ISBN 978-0-593-64731-8 (ebook)
Printed in the United States of America
10 9 8 7 6 5 4 3

When Elton John was born on March 25, 1947, he wasn't Elton John at all. His name was Reginald Dwight. He lived with his parents, Sheila and Stanley, in his grandmother's house in a town called Pinner, near London, England.

Reg was an only child. He often felt awkward and shy, but one thing made him light up: music.

Reg's dad was a trumpet player. His mom listened to lots of records. Even as a little kid, Reg could hear a song once and know how to play it on the piano. He took lessons and practiced. His piano playing got better and better.

He got so good that the Royal Academy of Music in London gave him a scholarship when he was eleven years old. He went there to study music every Saturday.

Well, almost every Saturday. Sometimes he skipped out to buy records of his favorite rock stars. The academy taught him classical music, but Reg loved rock and roll!

At fifteen, Reg got a steady job playing the piano at a local pub. Sometimes the rowdy crowd sang along. Other times, they ignored him.

But Reg didn't mind. He just kept on singing.

As a teenager, Reg played in a band called Bluesology. After a few years, he saw an ad in a newspaper: LIBERTY RECORDS WANTS TALENT. They were looking for singers and songwriters.

Reg had talent! He could play piano and sing. He could write melodies. But he wasn't great at writing lyrics—the words to the songs.

Reg didn't get the job.

But a man at the record company handed him lyrics written by Bernie Taupin, who had answered the ad, too. Maybe together they could write something special.

Reg and Bernie hit it off right away.

Reg knew he wanted to make music forever. But he didn't feel cool enough for rock and roll. And his name didn't sound like a rock star. He needed a change.

He borrowed "John" from one friend and "Elton" from another. Just like that, Reg Dwight became ELTON JOHN.

Bernie became Elton's songwriting partner. Later, they even became roommates, sharing a room in his mum's house. Elton got the top bunk.

They made a great team. First, Bernie wrote the words to the song. Then Elton wrote the melody, sometimes while eating breakfast. He was that quick!

Elton and Bernie tried writing music for other people, but when their quirky songs didn't sell, Elton sang them himself. His first album came out in 1969. Hardly anyone paid attention to it.

Elton and Bernie kept trying. The more songs they wrote, the better they got. Elton soon recorded a second album.

That album changed everything.

The record company booked Elton at a popular club in Los Angeles, California, called the Troubadour. Famous musicians liked to hang out there. That night, some even came to hear him play!

Although he was nervous, Elton launched into his music. He stood up, kicked back his stool, and pounded on the piano keys. He rocked the place, and the crowd loved it!

After that, sales of the new album went way up. Elton and Bernie had a hit!

Elton loved the spotlight, but he felt hidden behind his piano. Other rock stars could carry their instruments while they moved around the stage. How could he make himself stand out?

He dressed in flashy clothing. He did handstands on the keyboard. He sat on the floor and reached up to play the piano keys. Elton knew how to grab a crowd's attention—and keep it!

Elton and Bernie made hit after hit. Elton went on tour, putting on shows in cities and countries all around the world. Radio stations played his songs. Fans wanted his autograph.

In 1973, he got a star on the Hollywood Walk of Fame. But Elton John wasn't just a star—he was a superstar!

Even though he was famous, Elton didn't take himself too seriously. He played one concert in a Donald Duck costume. For another, he sported a sequined baseball uniform.

He wore hats, feathers, platform boots, and
really big glasses! Nothing was too over the top.

After twenty years of rock and roll, Elton decided to try something new. He wrote the soundtrack for the Disney movie *The Lion King* with Tim Rice. One song, "Can You Feel the Love Tonight," won an Academy Award. Later, the movie became a Broadway show.

First music, then movies, then Broadway—Elton did it all!

In 1993, Elton met David Furnish, a filmmaker from Canada. They fell in love, got married, and had two kids, Zachary and Elijah. His family made Elton very happy.

Everywhere he went, Elton made friends. He danced with Princess Diana and sang with John Lennon. He—and his music—helped lift people up when they were sad or lonely.

Through it all, Elton and Bernie continued to write songs together. Elton said Bernie was the best friend he ever had.

Elton knew that, thanks to his fame, he could help a lot of people. He started a charity to support patients with AIDS, a disease that attacks the body's immune system. Every year, he holds an Oscar party to raise money for the Elton John AIDS Foundation.

The Queen of England even knighted him in honor of his music and charity work. Today, he is Sir Elton Hercules John.

More than just his name has changed since he was that shy, awkward kid. But one thing has stayed the same: when he plays music, Elton John lights up!

"The GREAT THING ABOUT ROCK & ROLL IS THAT SOMEONE Like Me CAN BE A STAR."